IMAGES
of America

AROUND
GREENE COUNTY
AND THE CATSKILLS

William S. Borthwick (1870–1951), Brownie camera in hand, photographed many rural and family scenes around Cornwallville. Such amateur as well as professional photographers have preserved much of the visual history of Greene County, New York.

IMAGES
of America

AROUND
GREENE COUNTY
AND THE CATSKILLS

Raymond Beecher and Harvey Durham
in conjunction with the
Greene County Historical Society

ARCADIA
PUBLISHING

Published by Arcadia Publishing
Charleston, South Carolina

Library of Congress Catalog Card Number: 2008926676

For all general information contact Arcadia Publishing at:
Telephone 843-853-2070
Fax 843-853-0044
E-mail sales@arcadiapublishing.com
For customer service and orders:
Toll-Free 1-888-313-2665

Visit us on the Internet at www.arcadiapublishing.com

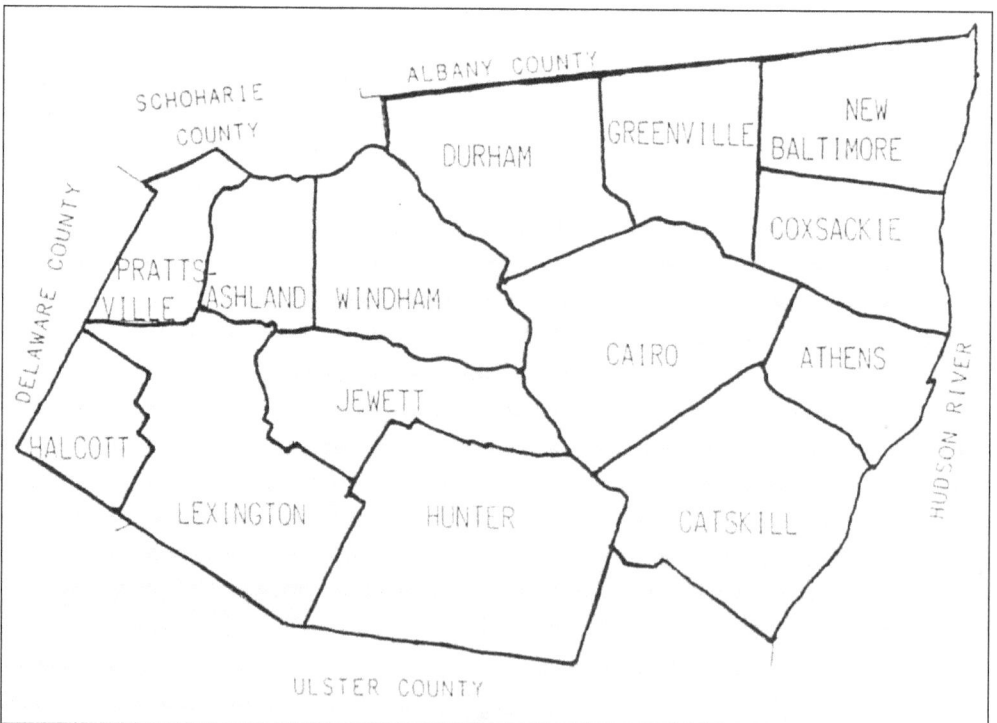

A map of Greene County, New York, showing the fourteen townships and neighboring counties. Greene County is bordered on the east by the Hudson River. The western portion is dominated by the scenic northern Catskills, which include Hunter Mountain with an elevation of over 4,000 feet.

Contents

The horses and trolley share unpaved Main Street, Catskill, at the turn of the nineteenth century. The brick building at left is still in use as a bank, having been chartered in 1813. At the right, the frame building with its permanent awning is presently used for real estate and insurance offices, while the second story houses a dentist's office.

The world-famed Catskill Mountain House, perched on a rock ledge 2,000 feet above sea level, gave visitors a spectacular view of the Hudson River 12 miles to the east. Built in 1823, it was remodeled and enlarged in later years. After a long period of decline, the dilapidated structure was burned to the ground by the state during the early morning hours of January 25, 1963.

Introduction

Whether of professional or of amateur status, photographers with Greene County connections have left their imprint on its local history heritage. Numerous examples of their skill with the camera survive in the photographic collections of the Vedder Memorial Research Library, an adjunct of the Greene County Historical Society. This visual image volume of Greene's events, places, and persons draws heavily upon those holdings.

Bordered by the Hudson River on its easterly side and incorporating the northern Catskills in the opposite direction, Greene County encompasses some of the most picturesque scenery in the eastern United States. By act of the state legislature, this county was established March 25, 1800, taking its name from General Nathanael Greene of Revolutionary War fame. Prior to 1800 its major land area was part of the original county of Albany and a minor part of Ulster.

The river valley and uplands east of the Kalkberg (Lime Ridge) attracted the prehistoric Native Americans who, in their different stages of development, gradually assumed a more settled pattern of living. The earliest Dutch-English land patents lay claim to this more fertile acreage and here the earliest European settlers established themselves with their families.

The New Netherlands period was relatively short, the area coming under English control about 1663. Although descendants of those early settlers were separated in their loyalties to the English Crown, the majority supported the concept of local political control and were allied with the revolutionary efforts, which eventually led to independence. Fortunate in escaping the direct ravages of war, the local residents provided quantities of supplies and manpower to the Revolutionary cause.

It was the Treaty of Paris in 1783 which finally established a climate of state expansion and one which opened the flood gates to settlers. The availability of much freehold title land on very moderate financial terms brought an influx of families from New England and from the lower reaches of the Hudson Valley. The small family farm of one hundred or fewer acres became the established pattern for Greene County. Waterpower from its numerous creeks and streams provided a modest industrial base.

Hudson River trading stations developed after the Revolution, ones which served for the shipping out of agricultural, forest, and manufactured goods. At one time Madison (Leeds) had the largest flouring mills in the state of New York. These river landings also served for the importation of manufactured goods, both domestic and foreign. The ancient Kings Road of 1710 was gradually superseded in importance by several turnpikes such as the Susquehanna, the Albany and Greene, and the Schoharie.

An abundance of clay and cheap water transportation to metropolitan areas encouraged the production of building brick. Until the hemlock bark was exhausted, the tanning of hides helped the county's economic well-being. Some farmers saw potential in fruit orchards. The opening of the Erie Canal was an economic blow to Greene County, one from which it was slow to recover. *Spafford's Gazetteer* had been overly optimistic in predicting that Catskill, the county seat, would in the decades ahead become the second or third major city on the banks of the Hudson.

Fortunately for Greene County, as its agricultural base declined in importance, the resort industry came into being. While the Catskill Mountain House preceded the Civil War era, and small hostelries provided lodging and food for travelers and artists, the major building boom for the medium and large hotels came later in the nineteenth century. Farmhouses generally catered to family units. Year by year the physical structures expanded to accommodate more boarders. The Hudson River passenger steamers as well as the railroads provided fast, inexpensive transportation. Finally, the advent of the gasoline-powered automobile coupled with improved roads insured a steady clientele. Skiing, a winter sport for the more active individuals, transformed the Mountain Top into a year-round resort operation.

In addition to the permanent population in Greene County, who earn a livelihood by commuting, etc., numbers of families retire to Greene County from the metropolitan areas while others utilize their properties on weekends. The county has not been immune to the changes affecting lifestyles elsewhere. Yet its rural, slower pace of life offers much to those who come here.

The authors are very grateful to the various individuals who have deposited personal and family photographic collections with the Greene County Historical Society. Appreciation is expressed to Kathleen Durham for the preparation of the manuscript for publication.

One

By Water and Rail

The replica of the *Half Moon* arrives at Catskill Point during the 1909 Hudson-Fulton Celebration. Local residents dressed in period costume surround Henry Hudson and crew. The Prospect Park Hotel can be seen in the distance.

Built for the Hudson-Fulton Celebration of 1909, the steam-propelled *Clermont* illustrates Robert Fulton's vision of the practicality of steam navigation on the Hudson River between New York and Albany. The success led to the rapid growth of river traffic, thus enhancing the economic prosperity of both valley and Mountain Top areas.

Few river landings were busier with the scheduled arrival and departure of day and night boats than Catskill Point. Station wagons from the hotels and boarding houses crowded the dock. Note the large paddle wheel in the center of the picture and the walking beam above the top deck.

The *Walter Brett* and the *Catskill* are docked below the iron swing bridge in Catskill Creek. A pile driver on a barge is located between the two night boats. This photograph predates the construction of the present courthouse on Main Street. Recognizable are the tall steeple of the former Baptist church, the old courthouse cupola, and the mill building north of the bridge.

The *Onteora*, 1898–1936, with a length of 236 feet, was built for the Catskill Evening Line for service as a night boat on the Catskill-New York run. This sidewheeler was destroyed by fire on September 21, 1936, while moored at Bear Mountain. In the background, from left to right, are such Catskill landmarks as the steeples of the Episcopal, Presbyterian, Baptist, and Catholic churches. The old courthouse cupola is at the right of the *Onteora*'s smokestacks; the armory is partially hidden by the vessel.

The *George H. Power*, a double-ended sidewheeler ferry, operated between Athens and Hudson for many years. On September 3, 1905, she collided with the "water taxi" *Young America*, resulting in the loss of four lives. The latter was raised and renamed the *Ramona*. Until the completion of the Rip Van Winkle Bridge in 1935, horse ferries and subsequently steam vessels serviced the three river landings of Catskill, Athens, and Coxsackie.

The *Isabella*, a 66-foot steam-powered "water taxi," plied the river between Catskill and Hudson. The boat was built in 1883 at the Magee and Van Loan shipyard at Athens. Captain Rainey named his infant daughter after his beloved boat. Miss Isabella Rainey taught elementary school in the Upper Village of Athens for forty-five years and lived to be one hundred.

12

Steaming out of Catskill Creek, the *Isabella* rounds Hop-o-nose, a famous natural landmark of fact and fiction. The creek was lined with ice houses, clay and shale brickyards, and textile factories which provided extensive employment.

The steam derrick *Reliance* struggles to raise the *Emeline* in Catskill Creek after she struck a rock opposite Hop-o-nose on a dark and rainy night in September of 1893. She was returning volunteer firemen to Poughkeepsie and Hyde Park from a firemen's convention in Catskill. Fortunately, no lives were lost in the accident. The vessel was built in 1857 and continued to operate until 1917, when she was crushed by ice while laid up for the winter at Haverstraw.

13

Towed excursion barges such as the *Andrew M. Church* earned owners income by carrying both people and baled hay. This barge, built at New Baltimore in 1891, frequently transported church groups and lodges to such amusement places as Baerena Park at Coeymans.

The *Norwich*, 1836–1920, a steam-powered workhorse, was used as passenger boat, freighter, tug, and ice breaker during her long eighty-four-year career. When she participated in the Hudson-Fulton Celebration of 1909, her paddle boxes were painted with the slogan, "Oldest Steamboat in the World." Her rugged construction and iron sheathing made her especially useful for ice breaking on the Hudson, earning her the nickname "Ice King."

The Hudson-Athens Lighthouse was built in 1874 and ceased operation in 1954, except for an automated light and fog signal. The last lighthouse keeper was Emil J. Brunner of Athens who retired from lighthouse service on May 30, 1949. The Hudson-Athens Lighthouse Preservation Society is restoring this historic structure with the goal of opening it to the public as a museum.

The river terminal of the Catskill Mountain Railway at the Point was where passengers boarded the trains for transportation to the mountain resorts. The maintenance crew serviced the rolling stocks in the large shops. Much of the area to the left has been filled in and is now a park known as Dutchmen's Landing.

15

The second Charles L. Beach locomotive on the Catskill Mountain Railway replaced an identical one of the same name and number that was destroyed by fire when the railroad repair shop at Catskill Point burned on December 7, 1908. Charles L. Beach was a major promoter and stockholder of the railroad, the Otis Elevating Railway, the Catskill and Tannersville, and the Catskill Mountain House, as well as other economic enterprises.

The Catskill Mountain Railway village station on Water Street was located a few yards south of Bridge Street. The State Armory was just to the left of the station. Though both buildings are now gone, the Holdridge quarry limestone retaining wall remains. The station was also the headquarters of the three Greene County railroads.

The West Shore Railroad was a major passenger and freight line from Weehawken to Buffalo, with scheduled stops at this Catskill Station near the high trestle bridge over Catskill Creek. The wood-frame building was destroyed by fire on December 6, 1909. It was replaced by the present heavy stone structure in 1912, which is no longer used as a railroad passenger depot.

This Catskill freight station, located westerly of the passenger station, was a busy West Shore depot, handling both incoming and outgoing freight. The style of architecture used in its construction was typical of the period.

The Catskill Mountain Railway train crosses the first bridge of the three that spanned Catskill Creek. The view, circa 1910, is from the high West Shore trestle. In the distance can be seen some of the buildings which housed the lumberyards, ice houses, foundry, and brickyards which contributed to a large part of the economic prosperity of the area. The first Catskill Mountain Bridge of 1882 still stands, but is now used as a pedestrian walkway and carries village water and gas lines.

The Catskill Electric Railway, later reorganized as the Catskill Traction Company, ran from Catskill Point to the flats just beyond the stone arched bridge over Catskill Creek at Leeds. The trolley first crossed in the year 1904. The two eastern arches of this historic Susquehanna Turnpike bridge were built in 1760. The attached wooden trestle at the west suffered repeated damage from spring freshets and was eventually replaced by additional stone arches in 1792. The aging structure was to be demolished and replaced by a modern bridge in 1936, but opposition led by Jessie Van Vechten Vedder, local historian, persuaded the state to number the stones before dismantling the bridge so that it could be restored to its original historic form.

After crossing the third span over Catskill Creek, the Catskill Mountain Railway stops at Gilligs Junction to pick up and discharge passengers. This stop was just below Vedder's Farm at Leeds Flats. The girl in foreground, near the post, is Mabel Vedder (Parks).

This work crew is posing on one of the Catskill Traction Company trolley cars. The arm at the top connects to the overhead electric line. The striped curtains, which could be closed in inclement weather, are drawn back in this photograph.

Locomotive No. 1 of the Catskill Mountain Railway is pictured here with crew members at the end of the line in Palenville after a run from Catskill Point.

In this image, construction is well underway at the summit of the Otis Elevating Railway, which was completed in 1892. A large stationary steam engine lifted and lowered two passenger cars between the base of the escarpment and the top by cable. The Catskill Mountain House was located a few hundred yards to the right and above Otis Summit Station.

One of the two seventy-five passenger cable cars provides a spectacular ten minute ride on the inclined track from the junction of the Catskill Mountain Railway at the base. A well-dressed brakeman at the right ensures added safety.

The two cars of the Otis Elevating Railway passed through four deep rock cuts and over three high wood trestles while lifting passengers 1,600 feet above Otis Junction. The total length of the rail was 7,000 feet.

Passengers board the Catskill and Tannersville Railway cars for the short trip to Otis summit, where they will descend the mountain on a cable car. From Otis Station at the bottom, they will take the Catskill Mountain Railway for their return trip to Catskill Point and the river boats.

Engine No. 4 of the Ulster and Delaware Railroad rests on the turntable at Kaaterskill Station, near the lower end of South Lake. The railroad line ran from Phoenicia on Esopus Creek through scenic Stony Clove to South Lake. A spur line ran to Hunter.

The large crowd waits for the next train at the Ulster and Delaware Railroad station in Tannersville. During the busy summer season, several trains a day were needed to transport the thousands of boarders who came to the Catskills.

Two

Over Roads
and Bridges

An early glass-plate photograph shows historic multi-arched Leeds Bridge, a noted Greene County landmark. It was constructed of native limestone, plentiful in the area. The Susquehanna Turnpike, which passed over this bridge, was a major thoroughfare westward to Unadilla on the Susquehanna.

A covered bridge was built by David H. Van Gelder at the natural dam site on Kaaterskill Creek. Just below the falls, a gristmill and Reid's pistol factory used the creek's waterpower.

This 1898 interior view of High Falls covered bridge illustrates one type of framework used to support heavily loaded horse-drawn wagons.

The Upper Town Bridge, spanning Catskill Creek, was supported by stone piers on Goat Island. This iron hoop bridge was replaced in 1906–1907 by a heavy concrete structure which presently carries Route 9W traffic.

The main crossing of the creek was at Bridge Street, in Catskill. In the fall of 1903, two men were drowned when high water swept away a section of the bridge. It has been replaced by two subsequent bridges named for "Uncle Sam" Wilson, who was once a resident of Catskill.

Construction is underway here on Webber Bridge (present Route 23A, west of the New York Thruway), in the township of Catskill. This arched span over the Kaaterskill is still in use.

In wintertime horses were harnessed to sleighs for both pleasure and commercial travel. The buffalo robes provided warmth while the string of sleigh bells provided a cheery sound.

Horses were the principal means of travel in rural areas before the advent of the automobile. The members of the Phinney family pose in front of their homestead, located between Freehold and East Durham. Note the working harness on the team. The lawn swing and large porch were typical of the late 1800s.

A sleek horse and light carriage furnish convenient transportation around Catskill village for Mrs. Paul R. Morrison, wife of a local professional photographer.

Wagons and carriages crowd the Cairo station of the Catskill Mountain Railway as they wait for the arrival of summer boarders during the summer of 1900. The numerous small boarding houses advertised transportation to and from their resorts. Railroad cars can be seen beyond the station.

Before the construction of the railroad line, elegant coaches were specially built for transporting well-to-do patrons from the boat landing at Catskill Point up the Mountain Turnpike to the lofty Catskill Mountain House. Leaf springs provided some measure of comfort as the wheels bumped over the rough and rutted roads.

An early automobile on Prospect Avenue in the village of Catskill foreshadows the momentous change from horse-drawn wagons to motorized vehicles.

An open touring car jounces along the muddy dirt road passing through Echo Notch on the way to Westkill in the Catskill Mountains.

The fear of runaway horses was replaced by concern about automobile accidents as motorized vehicles traveling on unpaved country roads became more common. This early accident occurred near Leeds.

Three

Earning a Livelihood

Agriculture was a major means of livelihood in Greene County. The hay crop was important for the farmer's livestock and was also a source of income when baled and shipped to New York by hay barges. This photograph shows the adjustable hay barracks sheltering the crop from the weather. At the right can be seen a horse-powered hay press and large bales beside it.

The Bronck farm, established in 1663, was one of the most prosperous farms in Greene County with hundreds of acres under cultivation. Several teams of horses and a number of hired hands were necessary to operate the farm.

A sturdy yoke of oxen drags a heavy stoneboat across a rough field. Stones from rocky fields were used for walls, foundations, and road fill. The photograph is from a glass negative taken by Paul R. Morrison, professional Catskill photographer.

34

The pre-Revolutionary Van Bergen mill, on Coxsackie Creek in the town of New Baltimore, is an example of the many local water-powered gristmills which served area farmers, who brought their grain to be ground into meal and flour.

Orville Smith's lumber and gristmills, store, and stone house were on Kaaterskill Creek at High Falls, town of Catskill. The cellar foundation for a new Smith house is in the foreground.

The Athens pottery works, located on Market Street, was operated by the Clark family for most of the nineteenth century. It produced quantities of stoneware that were shipped by water over an extensive area. Made for utilitarian purposes, these eye-pleasing products are highly prized by today's collectors.

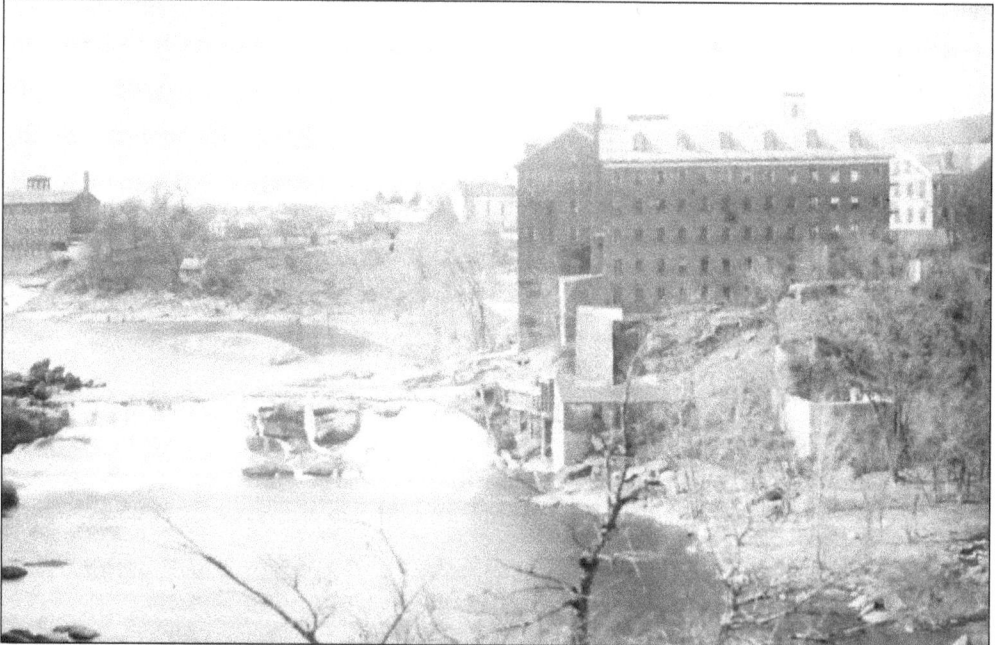

At one time this large Stewart mill complex on Catskill Creek at Leeds employed about 700 people for the manufacture of woolens, cloaks, robes, and other items. Today only the heavy stone foundations remain.

Ice harvesting on the Hudson River and creeks provided part-time employment during the winter months for many men and boys. Those with teams could earn extra money. In this photograph, horses and men are marking one of the ice fields in Catskill Creek.

This Hop-o-nose ice field near the mouth of Catskill Creek has been scored in preparation for harvesting. The knitting mill in the background furnished employment for both men and women.

This alert horse and enclosed home delivery wagon belonged to Ferdinand Ritz, whose grocery store was located in the Dolan Opera House Block, South River Street, Coxsackie, circa 1900. The light harness was adequate for this type of wagon.

Proprietor Charles Trowbridge, with clerks wearing white store coats, stands with a home delivery horse and wagon in front of his fancy grocery store, Main Street, Catskill.

This teamster came down the mountain to Catskill with his three-horse team weekly to deliver produce and return with a heavy load of merchandise to the Windham area. He routinely stopped to set his watch by the large clock in Willard's Jewelry Store on Main Street so as to return to the mountain top with accurate time for local residents. He froze to death in a later accident.

This is a typical turn-of-the-century grocery store, operated by the Ferdinand Ritz family in the Dolan Opera House Block on South River Street, Coxsackie. The store was later relocated to Reed Street. Note that the last letter of the store's name is reversed.

This two-chair barber shop was at Hotel Walters, in Cairo. The early-twentieth-century interior scene shows personal shaving mugs and brushes, cuspidor, Edison phonograph, lamps, and pictures of male interest. "Shaving 10¢ and Bay Rum 5¢."

The long-vanished typical meat market is illustrated by the Bloom family's business in Catskill. Sawdust was common on the floor. Smoked hams were hung from hooks but perishable meats had to be kept in the walk-in cooler at the rear.

The DuBois Pharmacy was once known as the oldest continuously operated drug store in the state of New York. Its marbletop soda fountain with hinged stools was a popular Catskill attraction.

This image shows an interior view of the Ritz Grocery Store at its second location on Reed Street, in Coxsackie. Freshly baked goods are on display in the glass counter. Open baskets, barrels, and boxes offer unpackaged merchandise.

This rural general store and post office was long operated by the Blenis family in the hamlet of Surprise, on Route 81 between Coxsackie and Greenville.

William C. Latta, wearing his leather apron and holding the tools of his trade, stands outside his blacksmith shop in Cornwallville.

This photograph of James Yeadon's blacksmith shop, across from the Round Top Church, presently the site of the firehouse, was taken circa 1905.

An attorney of one of the oldest law firms in Catskill is seated at his rolltop desk with telephone nearby. A framed law degree hangs on the wall. Cuspidors were common during this period of time.

The workmen and officers of the Athens Ship Building Corporation, North Water Street, Athens, pose for their photograph on June 29, 1918. The company made life rafts for the World War I war effort. This site was later the location of the Brady Steam Laundry, which was destroyed in an extensive waterfront fire on March 23, 1935. Following the fire, Brady built a new laundry building at the corner of Market and Washington Streets.

"Amos Post's Automobile Repair Shop and Agency for Overland, Franklin and Cadillac Cars" was on Church Street, in Catskill, circa 1915. The employees stand outside the building, which was formerly St. Luke's Episcopal Church, designed by famous Hudson River School artist Thomas Cole, a member of the congregation.

This selection from the camera of photographer Paul R. Morrison shows the process for building and launching large reinforced concrete barges at the L.B. Harrison Shipyard located on the Hudson River, north of Murderers Creek at Brick Row, Athens, between the Oil Dock Icehouse and the plant of the Composite Metal Lath Company. The icehouse, shipyard, and metal lath plant are long gone. Today, a restaurant and marina are in business just south of the former site of the shipyard. Here workmen fasten steel rods in the early stage of construction of a concrete barge, also known as a float.

This photograph from the Morrison series shows wood forms in place, ready for the pouring of cement over the steel rods.

The concrete railroad car float *Lake Champlain* is ready for a side-launching at the L.B. Harrison Shipyard in Athens on June 13, 1919.

Mrs. A. Post and W.P. Scully celebrate the launching of the concrete float *Lake Seneca* on October 28, 1919, at Athens, while guests and workmen watch.

The Alsen Cement Company at Alsen and the other two plants in the township of Catskill furnished employment for many area men. The West Shore Railroad and the nearby Hudson River provided convenient transportation. This plant became obsolete and has been closed.

Steam shovels load large rocks blasted from the Alsen limestone quarry into dump cars that are hauled by steam locomotives to the processing mill about 1917.

This photograph shows a part of the process used in converting limestone into cement at the Alsen Plant.

The overhead crane moves barrels of cement from the railroad flatbed to the barge in the Hudson at Alsen. Waterways were the cheapest transportation for such heavy products.

The Dairymen's League Co-operative Association, Plant No. 802, was located on Depot Street, in Catskill. Large quantities of Greene County milk were processed at this location near the West Shore Railroad.

Workers pose in front of the Catskill plant of the Dairymen's League about 1944.

Glass milk bottles are conveyed to the mechanized washer for cleaning and sterilization at Catskill.

Bottles were automatically filled, capped, placed in crates, and moved by conveyor for shipment.

Employees responsible for the local delivery of Dairymen's League milk were photographed at their garage on lower West Bridge Street, Catskill, on April 20, 1944.

Four

Resort Industry

The New Hart Hotel was located at Catskill Point near the ferry slip, the Hudson River Day Line dock, and the terminal of the Catskill Mountain Railroad. The trolley line to Leeds also started here. This building later became Loud's Hotel, which burned to the ground with all its contents on December 15, 1915.

Prospect Park Hotel in Catskill was at the end of Prospect Avenue and Harrison Street. It was an upscale summer resort hotel commanding spectacular views of the Hudson River to the east and the Catskill Mountains to the west. It was later sold and became Saint Anthony's Seminary. Total destruction came by fire in 1914.

The Malaeska House, located at South Cairo, was one of many similar summer boarding houses catering to families seeking cool fresh air, pure water, and a restful atmosphere.

The Catskill Mountains loom over Winter Clove House in the southern part of the township of Cairo. It was later expanded into a four-story wood-frame structure. Walking for pleasure was a daily routine of the summer vacationers.

On the road to Palenville in the 1890s, V. Branson's Glenwood Hotel was a resort complex of three buildings connected by a long spacious veranda. The amusement hall at the left provided indoor recreation, while the plentiful supply of porch rocking chairs allowed for outdoor relaxation.

This photograph shows a much enlarged Winter Clove House, an indication of the popularity of this summer resort. Unlike many boarding houses of its day, it continues in operation by catering to the interests of present-day patrons.

C.O. Bickelmann's Souvenir & Photography Studio at Tannersville is shown here about 1880.

Souvenirs of shaped and rustic wood were made and sold by E.B. Howard at his wood-turning shop in Tannersville. The small decorative display building is in sharp contrast to the lumber shed at the rear.

Martin's Hotel, formerly Roggin's Mountain Inn, was situated at the Four Corners in Tannersville in 1902. The striped post indicates a barbershop in the basement.

An early photograph shows Van Pelt's Hunter House in the Mountain Top community of Hunter. The covered omnibus and wagon standing in front of the two-story veranda are being watched by a number of guests.

Twilight Park, an exclusive summer cottage retreat for professional and artistic people from the metropolitan area, was one of several such parks. Its spectacular location near the hamlet of Haines Falls afforded views of High Peak and Round Top above and the famed Kaaterskill Clove below. The forest has since reclaimed the rocky pasture land.

Summer residents rest during their recreational walk at the private road entrance to Twilight, Sunset, and Santa Cruz Parks about 1914. The wood bridge over Kaaterskill Creek has since been replaced by a stone arched structure.

A boy and his donkey cart deliver private mail to residents of Onteora Park near Tannersville.

Relaxed guests enjoy the view from the ledge fronting the Catskill Mountain House about 1892. The thirteen Greek-style columns were a distinguishing architectural feature of this famed hotel.

An early automobile and an enclosed carriage share the grounds at the rear of the Catskill Mountain House about 1910. North and South Lakes are just out of view to the left of the picture.

The Hotel Kaaterskill, built by George Harding, was opened to the public June 28, 1881. From the beginning it was a strong competitor to the older Catskill Mountain House. Its guests arrived at Kaaterskill Station near South Lake and were then transported by coach to the hotel at the summit of South Mountain. The giant hotel was lost to fire the evening of September 8, 1924.

Kaaterskill Falls, with its drop of 260 feet, dictated the location of the Laurel House. Expanded from a plainer, much smaller building, it was a less expensive rival to its nearby neighbors, the Catskill Mountain House and Hotel Kaaterskill. Its deteriorated condition and the purchase of the site by the State Department of Conservation for park expansion doomed this structure to demolition by fire on February 27, 1967.

Many of the smaller hotels, like Gaffney's at Lexington, catered to the less affluent among the thousands of boarders attracted to the Catskills during the summer months.

Five

Scenic Views

This image is looking up Catskill's Main Street in winter, about 1910. Streets were left unplowed or were rolled for horse-drawn sleighs.

This is a view from Grant House piazza at Jefferson Heights about 1890, later the site of Greene County Memorial Hospital. The iron hoop bridge and the new West Shore Railroad bridge span Catskill Creek. In the distance can be seen Prospect Park Hotel on the west bank of the Hudson.

The Catskill Mountain Railway Bridge and the West Shore span are upstream in the village of Catskill beyond the iron swing trestle bridge. Brickyard sheds are in the foreground. At the right may be seen the old armory and the Catskill Academy, built in 1869 and destroyed by fire on March 8, 1935.

The natural dam on Kaaterskill Creek is shown here with the gristmill and Reid's Pistol Factory, which manufactured the famed "knuckle duster."

Just above the natural dam is David Van Gelder's long covered bridge at Kaaterskill Creek.

This image looks east on Main Street, Leeds, where the dirt road passes the Reformed Dutch Church built in 1818, the oldest church edifice still in use in Greene County.

High Falls, on the Kaaterskill near the Ulster County line, was one of many scenic falls visited by summer boarders.

This early view shows the village of Palenville at the entrance to Kaaterskill Clove, circa 1860s. The present roadway follows the course of the old turnpike to Haines Falls and Hunter.

Moore's Bridge on the Kaaterskill is just above Palenville. This wooden bridge has been replaced at least three times. Profile Rock is part of the ledge in the background.

Pictured here is Profile Rock in winter, as ice clings to the shaded side of the deep Clove at Moore's Bridge.

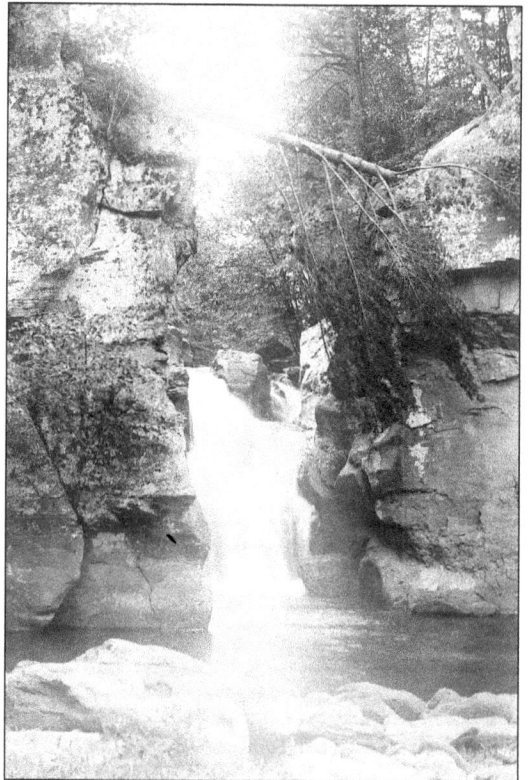

A few hundred feet above Moore's Bridge, Kaaterskill Creek tumbles over Fawn's Leap, one of the major natural attractions in the Clove.

A crude stairway leads to the observation platform on High Peak above Kaaterskill Clove, where visitors can, for a fee, gain a panoramic view of the Hudson Valley.

This is a rare view of the 150-foot-high Haines Falls from the bottom of the now nearly inaccessible stream bed. A wooden stairway once allowed easy access to the base. This photograph was taken during an unusual flow of water.

The Rip Van Winkle House, also known as the Halfway House, provided a welcomed rest stop for the coaches and passengers on their way to the Catskill Mountain House. The steep and narrow twisting road was a hard pull for the horses.

Hikers rest on the rocks above North and South Lakes. In the distance may be seen the top of the Otis Elevating Railway Station just below the Catskill Mountain House. At the right, Hotel Kaaterskill stands on South Mountain below the silhouette of High Peak.

Kaaterskill Falls, the highest falls in the state of New York at 260 feet, drops in two tiers, one of 175 feet and the other of 85 feet. The stream from North and South Lakes continues flowing over Bastion Falls at Horseshoe Curve on Route 23A and joins Kaaterskill Creek in the Clove below. The falls has been the inspiration for many artists, including Thomas Cole.

This well-worn plank stagecoach road passes through the forest near Palenville.

This view of Tannersville's unpaved Main Street looks westward toward Colonel's Chair. A large ski slope with many lifts at Hunter Mountain attracts thousands of winter sports enthusiasts.

A pedestrian swinging bridge spans Schoharie Creek near Hunter, with Colonel's Chair in the background.

This picturesque village street scene at Windham shows light pedestrian bridges on either side of Route 23, then unpaved.

Cleared hillsides overlook Ashland, situated along the banks of the Batavia Kill. As farming declined, trees gradually reclaimed the land.

The church, stagecoach inn, and general store are shown here along Upper Main Street, Ashland, about 1909.

This view shows Prattsville and Schoharie Creek in the Catskills. The placid stream in the foreground has a history of destructive behavior during spring thaws. The cluster of carvings in the cliff known as Pratt Rock is just out of view at the right.

West Kill is shown here on a branch of Schoharie Creek in the township of Lexington. A road no longer passable once connected with the adjacent township of Halcott high in the Catskills, the most westerly part of the county.

Six

Buildings Lost and Surviving

The Dutch architectural tradition survives in the National Historic Landmark Bronck Houses of 1663 and 1738 at Coxsackie. The rubblestone house at left is one of the oldest surviving dwellings in the state of New York. For family convenience, these two houses were connected with a hyphen hallway. The Bronck Homestead today is a museum and headquarters of the Greene County Historical Society.

One of three unusual barns on the Bronck Farm, this thirteen-sided structure with its single center pole for support attracts wide interest, especially from students of architecture. The interior platform looks down on the open below-ground level.

The structural design of the thirteen-sided Bronck Barn on the original Bronck Patent at Coxsackie is clearly shown in this image.

Lost by fire in 1929, the first Salisbury House of 1705 was constructed overlooking Potic Plain at Katskill, present-day Leeds. It was early known as "the mansion in the wilderness."

Old Stone House of Abeels, 200 Years Old.

The Abeel House, off Route 23A, in the township of Catskill, constructed of native rubblestone, survives in restored condition. It was the site of the Revolutionary War Tory-led Indian raid in which members of the David Abeel family were taken as captives to Canada in 1780.

This log cabin was built by pioneer Harlem Tompkins when he emigrated from Darien, Connecticut, to Old Windham's West Settlement. The photograph was taken in 1906. The cabin burned later but the cellar remains.

"Hush Hush," built by Fitch Lamphere for Major Augustine Prevost in 1792, is on Route 81 in West Greenville. It was the center of activity on the Prevost Land Patent which contained, among other buildings, a gristmill, miller's house, sawmill, potashery, and the Home Farm. Tradition has it that the name came from the almost oppressive stillness in the unsettled area.

This is an engraving of the Joseph and Charlotte Ely Sherman Federal-style homestead on the west bank of the Hudson River at the hamlet of New Baltimore. The four generations of the Sherman family who have lived in this house have helped shape New Baltimore's history.

Sadly, this interesting rest stop known as the Rip Van Winkle House has disappeared from the scene leaving only a few overgrown foundations. The opening of the Otis Elevating Railway in 1892 led to the abandonment of this stagecoach route to the Catskill Mountain House.

LEFT: This is an interior view of the old church at Kiskatom before the destructive fire. The second church was built on the same site and is still in use today.

RIGHT: The former Methodist Episcopal church at Greenville is shown here as it appeared about 1875. It still stands but is no longer used as a church.

This large commercial brick structure on the corner of Main and Bridge Streets, Catskill, survives as a two-story building as a result of a fire which destroyed the top portion. Law offices now occupy the ground floor of the former opera house building. The two steeples of the former Baptist church are visible at the left.

The construction of the present Greene County Court House at Catskill in 1908–1909 necessitated the removal of these buildings from the corner of Main and Bridge Streets to Clark Street. The tower of the Reformed church is seen at the far right.

The coal stove and the late Victorian clutter in the Catskill home of the DuBois family on Liberty Street presented a major cleaning problem for the housekeeper of that day.

83

This photograph from a glass-plate negative illustrates a well-to-do Catskill family bedroom. Today the furnishings and accessories are valued as antiques.

The historic brick Reger house at Second and Warren Streets, Athens, is in the process of demolition to make way for a grocery store. In turn, the new building became the temporary library for the Columbia-Greene Community College while that campus was being built near the east end of the Rip Van Winkle Bridge. At present it is the Athens Rivertown Senior Center.

Seven

Politics and Government

The new Greene County Court House at the corner of Main and Bridge Streets, Catskill, was open for public inspection on April 8, 1910. The separate jail and sheriff's residence on Bridge Street is at the rear.

The memorial fountain *Justice with Scales*, on the front lawn of the Court House, was the 1910 gift of the Honorable William P. Fiero. It has since been replaced by a columned marble fountain honoring veterans of World War II, Korea, and Vietnam.

The main courtroom in the Greene County Court House appears here much as it does today. The jury box is at the right.

This is an example of the "behind the counter" work space of the Greene County Clerk's office in the courthouse. Note the fancy grillwork and oak-finished counter cabinets of the day.

"Teddy" Roosevelt, in the center of the picture, addresses a crowd on the steps of the Greene County Court House.

Dominic DeSantis, winner of a 1916 Woodrow Wilson presidential campaign bet, sits in the wheelbarrow to be pushed up Catskill's Main Street by loser Sisto Fontanella, who supported Charles Evans Hughes.

Eight

Military

Men of the 16th Separate Company, New York National Guard, pose for their photograph in 1890. Their headquarters was in the Catskill Armory on Water Street.

Lieutenant Van Gordon, company officer, and the men of the 16th Separate Company are in summer field training at Camp Smith, Peekskill, NY, in 1894.

Walter A.S. Honan and Edwin W. Knoll, 16th Separate Company, encamped at the State National Guard camp during the week of June 29–July 6, 1895.

LEFT: Catskill men in training at Greenville, SC, during the Spanish-American War, get the news from home from *The Recorder*, their hometown newspaper.

RIGHT: Members of the 16th Separate Company of Catskill become Hudson Valley Champions for the basketball season of 1901–1902.

Catskill's ivy-covered National Guard Armory provides a backdrop for this group photograph of the 16th Separate Company, commanded by Donald Heath at far left.

Pictured here is a World War I rally, with soldiers standing in front of the Greene County Court House and backed by Junior Red Cross workers displaying signs urging support for French orphans.

In late 1930s, the marching band of American Legion Post 110, Catskill, posed in front of its headquarters on Green Street.

Nine
Gaining an Education

Principal James V.D. Ayers stands
with the faculty of the Catskill
Academy, off Thompson Street, in
the mid-1880s.

The student body and teachers pose in front of Durham's District No. 12 schoolhouse.

Cairo High School students have their group picture taken in 1922.

The second Academy Building, now the public library, provides a backdrop for the Greenville High School students in 1923.

Shown here is the student body of Prattsville Academy, Main Street, Prattsville. The building still stands minus the upper floor and galleries and presently houses the town hall.

The Catskill Free Academy and Grammar School, later the Catskill High School, was constructed in 1869. In 1907 the Irving Elementary School was constructed adjacent to it. The academy burned on March 8, 1935.

Ten

Recreation of Local Residents

Bicycling became a popular adult outdoor leisure activity from the 1890s well into the turn of the century. The frames of the ladies' bicycles were shaped to accommodate the long skirts of the day.

Cole's Grove, situated on the Hudson one mile above Catskill Landing, was unsurpassed for excursions and picnics. No intoxicating drinks were allowed by proprietor Theodore A. Cole. The donkey rides were an added attraction for children.

Cole's Grove beach, bathing houses, and picnic pavilions overlook the Hudson River at Catskill.

Many Greene County towns had their own community bands such as the Tannersville Cornet Band. They provided music for picnics, parades, and other celebrations and were frequently invited to play at events outside the county.

Several brothers of Coxsackie's Ritz family organized a brass band around the turn of the nineteenth century. It had a well-merited reputation throughout the area and was in frequent demand during the summer season.

Ice skating on the Hudson was a popular winter activity for both adults and children. This photograph shows a frozen Hudson under ideal skating conditions. Ice boating was also enjoyed by the more daring local residents.

Family and friends enjoy a picnic lunch on the Greene County Fairgrounds at Cairo on July 27, 1890.

The fall season brings out local hunters at Camp Hearts Content, Lawrenceville. The fields and woods offered hunting opportunities for big and small game and the shared sporting activity provided male camaraderie.

Members of the Athens Band take a traditional pose behind their bass drum. Few towns now support such local musical groups.

Trout fishing in Kiskatom Brook provides a family outing for the Frank H. Kortz and the John Cumming families.

Local youth could enjoy indoor sports at the YMCA, Main Street, Catskill. This three-story building, erected in 1902, later became the Boys' Club. The top floor was lost to fire but the building is still in use as a youth recreation center.

The Nelida Theater on Main Street, Catskill, brings out a large 1912 crowd. It was named for Nell Betts and Ida Warren, wives of the owners. Besides being used as a theater, it provided a roller skating rink and space for high school graduation exercises. It burned during the early morning of January 1, 1918, shortly after a New Year's dance, and was replaced by the present theater.

An early airplane, using the farm field as a runway, puts on a Sunday afternoon exhibition for interested Greene County residents. A free-will contribution was taken to cover the pilot's expenses.

Boaters enjoy an afternoon on Lake Rip Van Winkle at Tannersville. A swimming beach has replaced the boathouse at the left.

Cy Austin's "Easy Aces" dance band was one of many that played both summer and winter engagements. Dancing was a popular entertainment on weekends and drew large crowds.

Eleven

From the
Family Album

The family of Isaac and Ann Powell Smith is at Twin Oaks Farm on Earlton-Medway Road, about 1890. The original Powell homestead was constructed in 1790. Descendants are buried in the nearby family cemetery.

Millicent C. McCabe is pictured here at six months and twenty-one days, having been born on September 4, 1887. This daughter of Greenville's Dr. Charles P. McCabe had a short life span, dying on February 19, 1893.

A Palenville family poses for a tintype taken before the turn of the nineteenth century by longtime photographer Klitz, whose portable studio can be seen at the far right.

The Saxe brothers, sons of Christian and Rebecca Saxe of Catskill, sit for their family portrait at a reunion in Whitewater, Wisconsin, on May 21, 1885. They are, from left to right, Wesley, Wilbur, John, Stephen, and Ezra.

Edward Ely Sherman, at two years and three months of age, is shown here in July 1892. This well-dressed boy was a fifth generation descendant of Paul and Bathsheba Sherman. Paul was a noted sloop builder and trader in the hamlet of New Baltimore.

The Borthwick-Sanford families assemble about 1905 for a photograph at the Sanford homestead, Hervey Street settlement, in the town of Durham. William S. Borthwick (1870–1951) stands at the far right. He was a schoolteacher, historian and diarist, amateur photographer, and a member of the County Board of Supervisors (see also the frontispiece).

Marion Bloom of Catskill, born January 9, 1905, sits attentively for her photograph in a fancy wicker chair.

"Uncle Bronk Van Slyke" of New Baltimore sits on a rustic bench, his two daughters, Lena and Bertha, standing beside him.

Almyra Van Bergen (8/20/1827–8/20/1874) was the wife of Edmund Henry Van Orden. She was the great aunt of Edward Ely Sherman of New Baltimore, who is shown as a child in a previous photograph.

The Newkirks with their horse and dog pose in front of their Sandy Plains homestead near Leeds.

Visiting Niagara Falls are Augustus Sherman and his wife, Anna Van Slyke, on July 8, 1897. He was a lawyer, County District Attorney, and eventually the first secretary of the newly created State Prison Commission. His tragic death on October 7, 1898, was the result of a fall while disembarking from a river boat to the dock near his home in New Baltimore.

This Van Vechten family reunion took place at their homestead near Leeds, about 1897. Jessie Van Vechten Vedder (third person from the left in the back row) was one of the founders of the Greene County Historical Society, a noted author and historian, and the first appointed Greene County Historian. The society's Vedder Memorial Research Library is named in her memory.

The matriarch, Mrs. John A. Sullivan, who lived to be ninety-two, is at the family home on the corner of Thompson and New Streets, Catskill. She is the mother of Gertrude Sullivan Morrison, in the right background, wife of photographer Paul R. Morrison.

On the porch of "Al Vista," Thorpe Road off Route 385, Athens, well-dressed ladies with their embroidery hoops come together for a few hours of socializing on August 12, 1912.

Twelve

Group Activities

Flower booth attendants pose at the Dutch Kermess, which was sponsored by the First Reformed Church at the Nelida Theater, Main Street, Catskill, on January 14, 1903. Dressed in costume and identified on the left are Bessie Plusch and Fannie Millington.

The Ashland Band entertains guests at the Sutton-Cook reunion on Claude Sutton's farm about 1900.

The Citizens Hook & Ladder Company of Tannersville is pictured here about 1904. The fire-fighting equipment was pulled by men using long ropes.

The F.N. Wilson Steamer Company of Catskill was organized in 1854. The brick and stone structure, which was also the village building, was erected in 1899 and was totally destroyed by fire with the loss of all equipment. This Main Street site is now a parking lot.

The Cornwallville Methodist Episcopal Sunday School class was photographed on January 11, 1908. This historic structure was later moved to the Farmers' Museum, Cooperstown.

Mrs. Calvin Borthwick's Cornwallville Methodist Church Sunday School class, nicknamed the "Busy Bees," is shown here on October 31, 1915.

Holding their trophies with pride, members of the Osborn Hose Company of Catskill are photographed after becoming champions of the Catskill Mountain League during the winter basketball season of 1929–30.

The Athens Boy Scout Troop 40 is in front of the Athens High School, First Street, Athens, about 1937.

Thirteen

Fire, Flood, and Storm

A brick barge was torn from its moorings by high water and jammed against Catskill Bridge, destroying the west section of the iron trestle structure on October 9, 1903. Two men were drowned.

The pile driver constructs temporary support for the Catskill Village waterline following the damage to the bridge on October 9, 1903.

A floating crane removes the damaged section of the Catskill Bridge and loads the twisted metal on a waiting barge. A temporary structure of wood at the west end of the bridge provides a crossing for pedestrians and horses and wagons.

A crowd collects to watch the volunteers fight the fire at Horton Brothers Livery, Main Street, Catskill, in 1913.

Large chunks of ice are stranded on a street near the railroad tracks in Tannersville after high water flooded the area. Men with long peaveys attempt to clear a passage along the street.

The sudden, unexpected death of Augustus Sherman, prominent citizen of New Baltimore, on October 7, 1898, following an accident, brought out many mourners to his funeral. Here his Masonic Lodge escorts the hearse along the hamlet's Main Street.

Townspeople watch as the funeral procession for Augustus Sherman, which included dignitaries, masons, volunteer firemen, and other organizations, pass his house just up the street to the right.

Fourteen

Celebrations

The Captain John Pindar Association's annual clambake was held at Catskill on September 6, 1902. A brass band provided entertainment. Many fraternal organizations held such outdoor gatherings.

Five young men celebrated "Old Home Week" at Catskill in 1908 by parading in their "hoss-power" car. Parade watchers could enjoy this spoof on the gasoline-powered automobile just coming into use.

Mounted dignitaries, a brass band, and an early automobile parade along Catskill's Main Street. The buildings decorated with bunting add to the festivities.

The 35th meeting of the New York State Pharmaceutical Association was held at the Catskill Mountain House in 1914. The resort provided both business and recreational facilities for the members and their families.

The Pruyn Drum Corps of Catskill steps off smartly from the ferry slip as spectators watch and the trolley car to Leeds stands ready to leave.

Osborn Hose Company No. 2 of Catskill parades at the Greene County Firemen's Convention in 1915 at New Baltimore. The Reformed church building is in the background.

This dress rehearsal is in preparation for a skit to be given at the Durham Presbyterian Church.

A policeman keeps traffic moving on busy Main Street in Catskill during "Old Home Week" in 1922.

People crowd Main Street, Catskill, in front of the County Court House in anticipation of the parade which will soon be passing by.

The Greene County Historical Society float adds to the festive celebration of the sesquicentennial of the village of Catskill on August 11, 1956. The village was incorporated in 1806.

This children's Christmas party at Athens was sponsored by Local 39, International Ladies Handbag, Pocketbook and Novelty Workers Union, A.F. of L., about 1939. The Kadin Brothers Pocketbook Factory was located by the ferry slip on South Water Street.

www.ingramcontent.com/pod-product-compliance
Lightning Source LLC
Chambersburg PA
CBHW080847100426
42812CB00007B/1951